21 G

Lena Louise

BookLeaf
Publishing

Presentation by *BookLeaf Publishing*

Web: www.bookleafpub.com

E-mail: info@bookleafpub.com

ISBN: 978-93-95784-93-1

First edition 2022

DEDICATION

*For Samuel and Richard, with the hopes
that one day you will love wholeheartedly.*

ACKNOWLEDGEMENT

I would like to acknowledge all the women in my family who have supported me throughout my life and helped me believe that I have the strength to make my dreams come true. My mother especially.

A special place for Tom Grace (in this book and in my heart), for holding the lantern at the end of every tunnel.

PREFACE

This book will take you on an emotional journey. Some of the poems touch on sensitive subjects so I would like to take a moment to include a warning for those with trauma. If you are struggling with trauma that relate to any topics that may be in these poems, please feel free to shut this book and speak with someone you trust. If this is as far as you are able to read, I hope that one day, further into your recovery, perhaps you could find warmth from these stories of strength and empowerment. Be gentle, your mind is far more valuable than you could imagine.

The First Girl

Mother lost long ago
Raised by brothers
Father tried but didn't know
Out of touch

A childhood spent dreaming
Princess gowns and mermaid scales
But reality crept in
Losing faith in fairy tales
Pretty dresses were not enough
Mothers can't be replaced with stuff

Sense of belonging just out of reach
As if it were on the highest shelf
Chasing the pieces of herself

A stranger in her own body
Her mind strong but sharp
Like a broken mirror in the dark

The Summer Girl

Spring breathed life into the summer girl
After a long quiet, a long stillness
The summer girl, her soul destined to fade by
April
Only to kiss Autumn for a sweet moment

The summer girl, touched the hearts of those she
met
Joy blossomed around her, smiles lit their faces
But April comes, her light extinguished
Her glow turned ice blue and frosty

And once again the summer girl was quiet and
still
Next spring may light her fire once more

The Lonely Girl

A tragic girl, never to feel the touch of a kind
hand
Who watches the timer, the flow of that sand
If the city were woods she'd hide within the trees
From poachers who say they aim only to please

Her heart still hopes for a feeling she felt
But her fur is rare and wanted for pelt
Lured out of the shadows, grabbed by the arm
Yet another man who 'will do no harm'

Her skin now kissed with the scars of regret
Memories faded to them, but you can be sure
she will never forget

The Sleepless Girl

Eyes closed, but always watching
Tired girl, never falling asleep
Sounds she hears keep her awake
Movement in the darkness

They appeared to her as if a dream
If not seen by others, could it be real?
But what was not real if real to her
Eyes heavy, caught in a moment

They visit again, she hears them whisper
This time the figure stepped closer
Touched her
And she melted away

The Wild Girl

There she sat, calm and quiet
A storm raging in the depths
Her soul was twisted, searching peace
Everything before her eyes burned down

She could have lived the suburbian dream
But her heart charged with fire
Refused to settle for less than chaos
Freedom was her one true desire

The Vanished Girl

An unfortunate soul born in the wrong time
In early years taught the old line;
Children, though seen, should never be heard
So often the phrase, 'hush little bird'

Raised to believe her voice was worth less
Assuming her words left unspoken were best
Slowly dissolved into the background
Her silence unnoticed, barely a sound

Never again were the ears of her peers
Blessed with her simple and sweet morning song
Her smile and warm eyes now quiet inside
But outstretched are her wings, ready to glide

Fly away songbird, time to be proud
You are now free, you can be loud

The Faithful Girl

Dewdrops fall when the sun rises
Fireflies light lavender skies
Such beauty in her surroundings
And every night she prays

She trusts in the guiding forces
Puts her faith in her God's plan
And those angels up in heaven
Who seem to always light her way

Afternoon warmth on the pebbles
The taste of an ice cream
All the wonders that she knows He made
To bring our lives some joy

With beads in hand she whispered words
Blessings for the ones in need
She asked him for forgiveness
Prayed she led a faithful life
And was thankful for His love

The Mountain Girl

Cold air, weightless hair
Tones of auburn and gold flicked suddenly
A refreshing whip against the numb of her cheek

Frost covered boots, slippery rocks
Too treacherous for others, not even a path
Yet she, fluent in the language of these
mountains
Every step taken with confidence

Not a soul for miles, her presence alone
And just as she reached the top of her climb
The valley below gasped a breath through the
fog
Green treetops emerged as if for her

Her eyeline with heaven
A view only angels are blessed to see
The mountain girl

The Young Girl

Young, careless
Thoughtless, free
Nothing in her head
These are some of the things that they say

But none of them could know her
They don't understand the pain
Of growing up in a home where adults
Bring you to your knees

At six she tried to run away
But had nowhere to go
When nine she had the police called
It was the only way
By twelve she started drinking
Nobody would even know
And fifteen found a place to stay
With other kids without a home

This girl had never known much of love or
kindness
She's not to blame, when the adults plainly failed
her
How can it be her fault
When the ones who should have loved her

And made her feel at home
Instead of kisses better, only offered salt

But since she left there is still hope, rebellious or
not
If the adults that she comes across could show
her some compassion
Her brain still has not finished growing, she still
has much to learn

So smile and show her kindness
If you see her sitting on the street
There is still hope for her young, wild heart
Time for happiness and girl to meet

The Rainbow Girl

Pins on her bags and bright coloured hair
A single earring, not even a pair
A gem on her cheek she got as a dare
Matters not, either way they will stare

She shows with her body what she feels deep
within
Pictures and drawings all over her skin
To represent breaking their version of 'sin'
Negative words she takes on the chin

Growing up she suppressed the feelings inside
Nobody knew, desperate to hide
Spent half her life quiet without any pride
But she's now taking vows with her new bride

The Travelling Girl

No concept of comfort zone
Feels most loved when she's alone
House on wheels feels most like home
She must be wanderlust prone

She spreads her feet out on the sand
A quiet dance, a pink salt pan
Behind the wheel, without a plan
Stops to kiss a fisherman

Immersing in the culture, of anywhere she goes
The girl who comes from nowhere, teaching as
she grows
Seeking the impossible, proving she is brave
Vows to take but memories with her to her grave

A student born in nature, school is in the trees
Instead of class with teacher, she's listening to
the bees
Music taught by birds, science by the river
If it's learning that you want, nature can deliver

And when feels she's learned enough
Packs her van and all her stuff
No goodbyes, oddly enough
A girl who travels, must be tough

The Dancing Girl

She took her place in centre stage
Her body aligned with memories
Of movements echoed through mirrored walls
But curtains surround her now
Green velvet hung from her body, waiting
And suddenly, it began

Chaotic spins on a wooden floor
Hair flowing in the lights like golden thread
Hands twisting through the air like ribbons
Green velvet proving its loyalty
Pointed feet spoke beneath her
Singing the words in her heart
In a language understood by all
But spoken only by masters

The Skeleton Girl

Have you ever noticed what they sell to our
children
Brainwashed by the media that they have to be
thin
That skimpy is pretty, you must show your back
And the smallest size is always first on the rack

The girl in this story noticed all too well
Bought into the 'summer body' they sell
It wasn't her fault, they are to blame
Only perfect people are gifted with fame

It all came to a delicate balance
The difference was all in a word
There was a definitive moment
When her pain could have been heard

But sadly it had passed, it was suddenly too late
Thoughtless words were all it took to seal her in
that fate
She spiralled into self loathing and then into
despair
And even when they noticed, they didn't seem to
care

Rock bottom came, she had a thought
The realisation hit with stealth
In the moment that she almost bought
An urn for mother's shelf

Then came the answers she had sought
It's time to focus on herself
From skin and bone she fiercely fought
Until recovered back to health

The Native Girl

More to the story than feathers and beads
Than paintings and dances, or baskets of weeds
Connection to earth, respect for the trees
Kindness and meaning, things they believe
Teaching with stories, morals and needs
Souls laid bare with each brushstroke or weave

But how things have changed with the passage
of time
Pieces of earth cut by fences, "mine"
A girl with a wish to connect through the loss
Rebirth of the knowledge that she comes across

Adorned with the relics of her history past
But the clothing she wears is all colourfast
Tirelessly tries, as best as she can
In a world where assimilation began

Stolen culture, laws had changed
With dishonor, caused great pain
Destroyed the peace, lands obtained
All the things they stood to gain

Ghosts of ancestors, standing beside
Whisper to her about cultural pride

Connections with a remaining tribe
Now understands the feelings inside

The markets were selling 'traditional pieces'
But not made of natural leathers and fleeces
Blue feathers and plastic, not made from the soul
Without deeper meaning can never be whole

Her voice weak among others because of her
skin
Easy to see they were not listening
"If ever you want to repay your debt.."
"Stop using my culture as a trinket"

The Stargazing Girl

A girl without self is a strange paradox
Worldly possessions escape her
No interest in normal life here on Earth
Misunderstood as quite dull

She's searching for magic she knows is out there
But all of her friends call her mad
Some day she will prove that galaxies breathe
That the universe is alive

No vanity in an innocent heart
All of her mirrors point skyward
Doesn't buy makeup or things for herself
But can tell constellations apart

Wishes one day she could travel to mars
Dreams of swimming in space
Staying on Earth is quite boring
The girl with her head in the stars

The Caring Girl

This girl, once a daughter
Now a mother of her own
She's holding babe in one arm
Making sure their clothes are sewn

She cares not for her hair
Styling no longer fun
No time for curls or colours
Only pins it in a bun

With so many babies
Her life is filled with joy
She matches all their clothing
Each with a special toy

Her favourite thing of all to do
Is bake a giant cake
She lets all the kids choose toppings
They throw them in the goo

Each day she wonders how she could improve
What she could do better
She doesn't know how proud we all are
These children won't forget her

The Garden Girl

Garden girl, golden fingers
Kisses the soil with a magic touch
Green surrounds her, a forest home for fairies
Some say she met a genie who granted her a
wish

She plants her soul with every seed
Sings to them in winter
The girl who wants to grow the world
Gives them everything they need

No worldly love, humans don't understand why
The wildlife are her family, they stand beside
She lives without waste, grows her own food
Trees she planted years before now touching the
sky

While everyone else owes Earth a debt
Garden girl living with nature, a peaceful life
she will never regret

The Old Girl

Aching, the end was slowly approaching
Endless memories once shared now held in her
mind alone
Her orange blossom china once a prized
possession
Now a play set when grandchildren stay
Oh how things have changed

Old girl, I wonder what beauty is in your mind
What incredible things you've seen during your
time
Old girl, I'm sorry we haven't loved you enough
I promise we'll cherish the films once you're
gone
Old girl, no more stories, or answers for our
questions
No longer in pain, now you can rest

The Butterfly Girl

Crispy red leaves crunched beneath her tired feet
Her golden hair lit softly by glowing berries
which adorned every branch above her
A carpet of moss with purple blossoms spread
along the edge of the path

The sweet song of a small round bird followed
her as she approached
A small puff of air kissed her cheek as a
butterfly passed her
She took a large iridescent petal in one hand,
touched the nectar to her lips

Blue wings tore through the back of her dress
and unfolded behind her
Her magic was restored, her soul replenished,
she was whole again, she was finally home.

The Broken Girl

Wings picked from a butterfly
The lion lost its roar
Girl, you'll never reach the sky
Girl, your throat is sore

This is just what happens
When one heart loves too much
And when it's clear you've had enough
Then comes a gentle touch

Girl, there's more in store for you
Than to become a battered wife
Girl, it's best to leave him
Before you lose your life

The Last Girl

He whispered 'Never!'
Before he left her alone
She did it anyway...